IN HER HANDS

THE STORY OF SCULPTOR AUGUSTA SAVAGE

by Alan Schroeder · illustrated by JaeMe Bereal

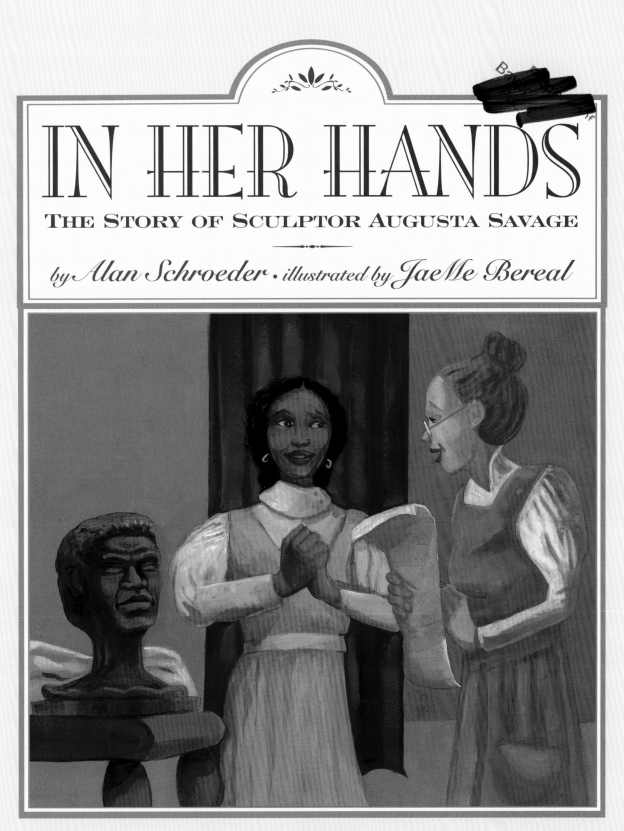

LEE & LOW BOOKS INC. NEW YORK

To Beverly Davis and Margaret Wilson, with love—A.S.

"Creativity is allowing yourself to make mistakes. Art is knowing which one to keep."
—Scott Adams

To my friend Michael Grefe who encouraged me when I was illustrating this book.
To all my friends and family who still love me, and to all those who didn't
know about Augusta, but will now, because of this book—J.B.

This story is based on the early life of sculptor Augusta Savage. Savage's life has not been well documented; therefore, some details and dialogue have been imagined to fill gaps in the historical record. The following sources were helpful to me in recreating Augusta's story.—A.S.

Leininger-Miller, Theresa. *New Negro Artists in Paris: African American Painters and Sculptors in the City of Light, 1922–1934.* New Brunswick, NJ: Rutgers University Press, 2001.
Bearden, Romare and Harry Henderson. *A History of African-American Artists from 1792 to the Present.* New York: Pantheon Books, 1993.
Low, W. Augustus and Virgil A. Clift. *Encyclopedia of Black America.* New York: McGraw-Hill Book Company, 1981.
Mabunda, L. Mpho, ed. *Reference Library of Black America.* (Based on the 7th edition of *The African American Almanac.*) Detroit: Gale, 1997.
Hine, Darlene Clark, ed. *Black Women in America: An Historical Encyclopedia.* New York: Carlson Publishing Inc., 1993.

Photograph of *Gamin* (p. 44) courtesy of the Smithsonian American Art Museum, gift of Benjamin and Olya Margolin. Photograph of Augusta Savage working in her studio on *The Harp* (p. 45) © Morgan and Marvin Smith. Reproduced courtesy of Monica P. Smith and the Schomburg Center for Research in Black Culture.

Text copyright © 2009 by Alan Schroeder
Illustrations copyright © 2009 by JaeMe Bereal

LEE & LOW BOOKS Inc., 95 Madison Avenue, New York, NY 10016
leeandlow.com
Manufactured in China
Book design by Christy Hale
Book production by The Kids at Our House
The text is set in Berkeley Book
The illustrations are rendered in acrylic
10 9 8 7 6 5 4 3 2 1
First Edition
Library of Congress Cataloging-in-Publication Data
Schroeder, Alan.
In her hands : the story of sculptor Augusta Savage / by Alan Schroeder ; illustrated by JaeMe Bereal. — 1st ed.
p. cm.
Summary: "A biography of African American sculptor Augusta Savage, who overcame many obstacles as a young woman to become a premier female sculptor of the Harlem Renaissance. Includes an afterword about Savage's adult life and works, plus photographs"—Provided by publisher.
ISBN 978-1-60060-332-7 (hardcover : alk. paper)
1. Savage, Augusta, 1892-1962. 2. Sculptors—United States—Biography. 3. African American sculptors—Biography.
I. Savage, Augusta, 1892-1962. II. Bereal, JaeMe. III. Title. IV. Title: Story of sculptor Augusta Savage.
NB237.S286S37 2009
730.92—dc22   [B]   2009003859

American sculptor Augusta Savage (1892–1962) was born and raised in Green Cove Springs, Florida. She was by nature a private person, and little is known about her life. In fact, she has been called one of the most enigmatic figures in American art. In this book, I have tried to present the facts of her early life accurately. I hope I have captured some of Augusta's spirit as well. As both an artist and a teacher, Augusta Savage was a central figure of the Harlem Renaissance; and though only a small fraction of her work survives, she deserves to be better known. —A.S.

Out back, behind the house, there was an open pit filled with clay—soft, gooey, just-waiting-to-be-shaped-into-something clay. Every afternoon, Augusta would sit barefoot at the edge of the pit and make little clay figures. Her mama, Cornelia, didn't mind, even if she did think it was messy. But her daddy, Edward, disapproved. He thought Augusta was wasting her time.

One afternoon, he came out to the pit and gave her a sour look.

"What's you doin' there, girl?"

Augusta held up her hands, sticky with clay. "Playin'. Makin' stuff."

"Playin'?" Edward shook his head. He was a preacher and didn't believe in play. "You ought to be reading the Bible instead," he told her, "cultivating your mind, saving your soul."

"I don't want to read the Bible," Augusta said stubbornly.

Edward grabbed her by the wrist and yanked her to her feet. "Don't you never talk back to me!" he said. And he gave her a sharp swat on the rear, so she wouldn't forget.

Twice a week the entire family had to go to church. Augusta and her sisters would put on their best dresses, and the boys their best pants, and Cornelia would take them down the road to church. The only part of the service that Augusta liked was the singing. After her father's sermon, the men and women of the choir would step forward and begin to sing. If Augusta was lucky, they would sing her favorite song:

> *He's got the whole world in His hands,*
> *He's got the whole world in His hands! . . .*

After church Augusta would hurry home and put on some grubby clothes. Then, plopping down next to the pit, she would sink her fingers into the wet, gooey clay. Nothing made her happier than to take a fistful of wet clay and turn it into a duck or a chicken or a little pig with a curly tail.

The whole time she lived in Green Cove Springs, Augusta made little clay figures. She gave some to her brothers and sisters, but mostly she kept them hidden at the bottom of her mama's trunk, where her daddy wouldn't find them. Edward didn't like to see them around the house—he called them profane—and if he found one, he would crush it to dust.

One afternoon, Cornelia went to draw water from the pump. Next to the shed, she found her daughter crying, clutching a smashed clay figure in her hands.

"He didn't have to step on it," Augusta kept saying. "He does it just to be mean."

Cornelia ran her hand through Augusta's hair. "No, he's not mean," she said. "He's just . . . he just doesn't understand, that's all. He'll come around, Gussie. Give him time."

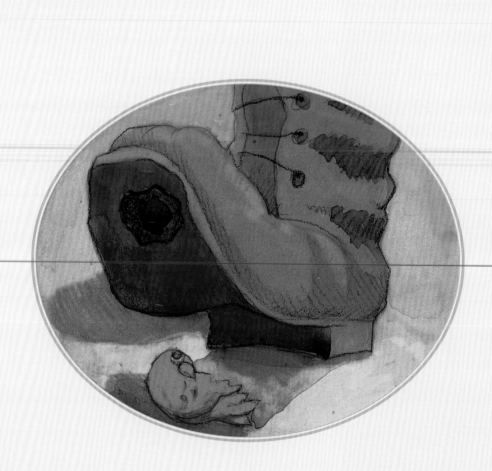

When Augusta was fifteen, Edward took a job at a church in the southern part of Florida. Augusta packed up her dresses and her shoes and her little clay figures and, with the rest of her family, she moved to West Palm Beach.

But she didn't like it there. There were no clay pits in town—none that Augusta could find, anyway—and for nearly a year she didn't make a single clay figure. Not one. Her heart grew heavy, and she wondered if she would ever work with clay again.

Then, one day Augusta was riding in a wagon with her school principal, Mr. Mickens, when she saw a sign in front of a shop:

CHASE POTTERY
FACTORY OPEN TO THE PUBLIC

Pottery, Augusta thought—that means clay! "Stop, stop the wagon!" she cried. "I've got to get out!"

Mr. Mickens drew the horse to a halt. "I'll be back in a minute," Augusta told him. Then, quickly, she ran into the factory. There was no one inside; but out back, under a battered tin roof, she found a long worktable, a potter's wheel, and buckets and buckets of clay. Augusta wondered where it came from.

"I have a friend up North. He sends it to me," the owner told her.

Augusta dipped her fingers into a bucket. The clay was soft and gooey, just like the kind she had known in Green Cove Springs. Only this clay wasn't red.

"Go on, take some," the potter said. "I've got plenty. But you've got to promise to show me some of your art sometime. Maybe I can learn something from you."

Augusta was surprised to hear him use that word, *art*. She had never thought of her pieces that way before. It was certainly something to think about. . . .

"You seem mighty happy," Mr. Mickens said when Augusta returned to the wagon.

Augusta nodded. "I've waited a long time for this day."

At home, Augusta showed her mother the three buckets of clay that Mr. Chase had given her. Cornelia looked worried.

"If I was you, I'd keep it out of sight," she warned. "It'll just make your father mad."

Augusta hid the clay—all twenty-five pounds of it—in the toolshed, under a feed bag. It wasn't long before Edward found it. He was all set to throw it out, but Cornelia begged him not to.

"Edward, I've never thought of you as a mean person before, and I don't want to start thinkin' of you that way now. Augusta ain't done nothin' wrong. You just let her be."

"But . . . but it's sinful!" Edward insisted.

Reaching over, Cornelia took the buckets away from her husband. "You go inside and wash up now," she said. "Supper's at five."

Augusta never found out what her mother had said to her father. But from then on, she was allowed to make as many clay ducks and chickens as she liked. One day, for fun, she sculpted something different: a Virgin Mary, eighteen inches high, with soft, folded hands and a face like an angel.

She took it to school, and when Mr. Mickens saw it, he was impressed.

"You've got real talent," he said, "and it shouldn't go to waste." He gave Augusta a kind look. "Tell me, how many brothers and sisters do you have at home?"

"Thirteen," Augusta answered, "plus me, and Mama and Daddy."

"That's a lot of mouths to feed," the principal said. He knew that Augusta's family was poor, and he wanted to help if he could. "I've been thinking," he went on. "If Mr. Chase is willing to give us some clay, I'd like you to teach the other students how to work it, how to make little figures like you do. If you do that, Augusta, I'll give you a dollar a day."

Augusta's eyes widened.

"Every day?" she whispered. She couldn't believe he had that much money.

The principal smiled. "That's right. Every day."

Edward didn't like the idea of Augusta teaching other children to waste their time. But he was sure quick to take the dollar that she brought home every day.

Long after Augusta had stopped going to school, she continued to make figures out of clay: dogs, cats, houses, people. She liked her work, but as time passed and Augusta grew up, she wondered if her sculptures were any good. It wasn't enough that her mother said so—she had to find out for herself. When Augusta was twenty-seven, she entered some of her clay figures in the county fair. On the day of the contest, the judges moved from table to table, writing in their notebooks.

Cornelia was sure that her daughter would win. "I've seen every entry," she told Augusta, "and, Gussie, yours are the best." Then Cornelia's voice dropped. "Don't tell your father I said so, but I really think you should become an artist."

The judges agreed, and Augusta won the twenty-five-dollar first prize. She also won a special ribbon for "Most Original Exhibit."

That evening in the moonlight, Augusta walked home with
George Graham Currie, the man who ran the fair. They had met
only a few days before, but already they had become good friends.

"I think your mama's right," Mr. Currie said. "Maybe you should
become an artist."

For several days, Augusta had been thinking the same thing.

"I could help you, if you'd like," Mr. Currie went on. "I know a
sculptor in New York. His name is Solon Borglum."

"Is he famous?" Augusta asked.

"Pretty much—even got his own school." Mr. Currie nodded. "I'll
bet if you were to ring his doorbell, he'd be glad to give you a hand."

When Augusta arrived home, she discovered her mother sitting on the porch. It was a warm night and Cornelia was fanning herself.

Augusta sat down beside her. "Mama, I've made up my mind. I'm gonna use the money I won to go to New York," she said. "I'm going to become an artist!"

Cornelia looked startled. "New York? But . . . but that's so far away! Ain't you scared?"

"Of course I'm scared. But if I don't do it now, I never will." Augusta took hold of her mother's hand. "Oh, Mama, be happy for me. That's what I need."

Cornelia wiped a tear from her eye. "I *am* happy for you," she said. "But, girl, I'm gonna miss you so!"

On a hot day in late September, Augusta took the train to New York City. As soon as she arrived, she found herself a little room in Harlem. Then she went to see Mr. Currie's sculptor friend, to ask if he would give her lessons. Solon Borglum was a nice man, but he shook his head.

"I'm afraid I charge ten dollars a lesson," he said. "Do you have ten dollars?"

The unhappy look on Augusta's face was all the answer he needed.

"Don't give up," he said. "There's an art school here in New York that doesn't charge any tuition. I'll write you a letter of introduction, try to get you in."

Mr. Borglum reached for a pen. Meanwhile, Augusta looked around the room. On every shelf there were sculptures of cowboys and Indians and bucking broncos.

"Are all these yours?" she asked.

The artist nodded. "Yes, indeed. Every one of them. I grew up in Nebraska," he said, "roping and riding. I've even lived on an Indian reservation. I guess you could say I sculpt what I know." He signed his name to the letter. Then he gave Augusta a curious look. "Tell me, Miss Savage—what do you know?"

Augusta was confused. "I don't know what you mean."

"Oh, I think you do." Mr. Borglum smiled. "What matters most to you? When you think about your life, what comes to mind?"

Augusta had never been asked that kind
of question before. She closed her eyes and
thought for a moment. Green Cove Springs—
that was what she cared about. The place where
she'd grown up, with its clay pits and its smelly
sulphur springs, and the school she'd gone to,
and all the kids she used to play with—Maisie and
Margaret and Pee-wee . . .

She thought of her daddy's church, and all the people who went there on Sunday to listen to him preach. She could see her daddy in her mind, up there at the pulpit, clutching the Bible and talking about Jesus and doing right and a glorious day sure to come. She remembered holding on to her mother's hand, while next to the pulpit, in purple robes, the members of the choir rocked back and forth, filling the church with joy:

> *He's got you and me, brother, in His hands.*
> *He's got you and me, sister, in His hands.*
> *He's got the whole world in His hands!* . . .

Augusta opened her eyes. Mr. Borglum was looking at her. How could she explain to him what she'd seen in her mind?

"You don't need to tell me," the sculptor said. "I could see it in your face." He folded the letter into thirds and slipped it in an envelope. "I hope this gets you in," he said, "but if it doesn't, don't come back. There's nothing more I can do for you."

The next morning, Augusta went to Cooper Union School and presented her letter to the lady in charge. Miss Reynolds was a tall, thin woman with her hair done up in a bun. She read the letter, then she handed it back to Augusta. "All right," she said, "where are your pieces? Show me."

Augusta was taken aback. "I don't have any," she said. "I mean, I do . . . but they're at home, in Florida."

Miss Reynolds frowned. "So you've brought nothing to show, nothing at all?"

Augusta looked at her feet. "I'm sorry," she mumbled. "I didn't know."

Miss Reynolds glanced at her watch. She had work to do. At the same time, she felt sorry for Augusta and wanted to give her a helping hand.

"Listen to me, Miss Savage. I want you to sculpt a piece for me tonight. I don't care what it is, or how small it is, but you bring it to me tomorrow morning. I'll decide then whether to admit you or not."

That evening, in her tiny apartment, Augusta unpacked a heavy lump of clay she had bought at an art supply store. Using a knife, she cut the clay into several pieces. What she had in mind was a barnyard scene. She had been sculpting ducks and chickens for years; they were easy to make. But would that be enough—a family of ducks? What would Miss Reynolds say when she saw them?

With a sigh, Augusta mashed down the duckling she had started. Then she remembered what Mr. Borglum had said. "Sculpt what you know." Augusta closed her eyes and thought deeply.

Church. Her father. The pulpit. Those long sermons. Those were the things that she knew best.

That very morning on her way to Cooper Union, Augusta had passed by a church. Through the open door, she'd seen a minister, standing at the pulpit, speaking to the congregation. A big man, with a wide, friendly face. Augusta tried to picture his features—his close-cut gray hair, the birthmark on his cheek, the gap between his front teeth.

It took a while for Augusta to fix the image in her mind. Then she took a deep breath, sank her fingers into the clay, and went to work.

Hours passed. In the apartment above, someone was playing the piano, a ragtime piece. Down below, a baby was crying. Out on the fire escape, Mrs. King was cooking hot dogs. But Augusta did not hear the piano or the baby; and though her window was open, she did not smell the hot dogs. All of her attention was given to the block of clay in front of her. That was the only thing that mattered.

Here and there, pockets of stars appeared in the sky. The piano had gone silent; the baby was quiet. Harlem was fast asleep. But in one third-floor apartment, a light continued to burn far into the night. . . .

Early the next morning, Augusta showed up at Cooper Union. She looked tired, as though she hadn't slept. In her hands she held something heavy, covered with a dish towel.

"Well, let me see it," said Miss Reynolds. "I haven't got all day."

Augusta placed her artwork on a nearby table. Then she removed the dish towel.

Miss Reynolds studied the sculpture with a critical eye. "Hmmm. . . ." At one point, she turned the bust around so she could see the back of it.

Minutes ticked by. Miss Reynolds jotted something in a notebook. Then she turned to Augusta. "Tell me, where are your parents?" she asked. "Are they here in New York?"

"No, ma'am, they're in Florida. That's where they live. My daddy's a minister."

Miss Reynolds nodded. "Well, you write to them tonight, and you tell them that their daughter is officially a student at the Cooper Union School of Art."

Augusta could hardly believe her ears. "You mean it?" she cried.

"You'll start tomorrow morning," Miss Reynolds replied. "Come to my office at nine o'clock. And you needn't bring any clay. We'll provide all your supplies for you."

Outside, as she stood on the steps, Augusta's heart pounded with joy. Ever since she was a little girl, she had dreamed of becoming an artist, and now that dream was about to come true!

At the bottom of the steps, something caught her eye—a hopscotch pattern on the sidewalk. Augusta laughed and, setting down the bust she was carrying, she began to skip lively.

> *Mabel, Mabel, set the table.*
> *Don't forget the red-hot label!*
> *Shake the salt and shake the pepper.*
> *Who will be the highest stepper?*

A group of students who were going into Cooper Union stared; a few even laughed. But Augusta didn't care. She felt too happy. Besides, she had to do *something* to celebrate.

With her eyes shut, she skipped back to where she'd started. She collected the bust that she had made, the one that had gotten her into Cooper Union. Then, half walking, half skipping, Augusta turned her steps toward Harlem, toward home. She had a letter to write.

Augusta Savage began attending classes at Cooper Union in October 1921. She worked hard—so hard, in fact, that she managed to complete two years' worth of study in just six weeks! Even though Cooper Union was tuition-free, Augusta was still responsible for her personal expenses: rent, food, and carfare. She had arrived in New York City with very little money—less than five dollars—and by February, she was broke. It looked as though she might have to return to her parents' home in Florida. But then, good fortune intervened. The administrators at Cooper Union voted to supply Augusta with the funds that she needed—a first for the school. In their eyes, she was an exceptional student who ought to be given as much encouragement as possible.

Their faith in her was not misguided. Upon graduating from Cooper Union, Augusta Savage went on to become one of New York's most promising artists, winning important commissions. The first of these was a portrait bust of civil rights leader W.E.B. Du Bois. She followed this with a likeness of black nationalist Marcus Garvey. Both busts were well received, the Du Bois especially so; for more than thirty-five years, it occupied a place of honor in the Harlem branch of the New York Public Library. But Augusta's most famous piece in the 1920s was *Gamin*, a bust of an African American boy with a cap set jauntily upon his head. A life-size bronze, *Gamin* has lost none of its appeal over the years—it continues to delight everyone who sees it.

In the early 1930s, Augusta Savage discovered that she had another talent—one for teaching—and she opened an arts and crafts studio in Harlem. From the start, her favorite students were children. Any time she saw a youngster lingering by the door or peering through the window, she would rush forward, crying, "Come in, come in!" Augusta had a knack for helping children discover and nurture their artistic ability.

Her success as a teacher was not overlooked. In 1937, she was appointed director of the Harlem Community Art Center, at that time the largest art center in the nation. Gradually, Augusta became convinced that if she was going to be remembered for anything, it would

Gamin, circa 1929

Photo courtesy of the Smithsonian American Art Museum, Gift of Benjamin and Olya Margolin

be for her teaching, not her sculpture. "I have created nothing really beautiful, really lasting," she said. "But if I can inspire one of these youngsters to develop the talent I know they possess, then my monument will be their work."

Her artistic career, however, was not yet over. In the late 1930s, she was asked to create a sculpture with a musical theme for the upcoming World's Fair in New York. She found her inspiration in James Weldon Johnson's "Lift Every Voice and Sing," a powerful composition considered the Negro national anthem. The piece that Augusta sculpted was remarkable: a harp, sixteen feet tall, the strings of which were figures of children, each with his or her mouth open in song. *The Harp* attracted many spectators when it was unveiled in 1939. Widely photographed and much discussed, it lent to Augusta's name a degree of prominence she had never before known. Fame, which had always proved elusive, was suddenly hers.

Sadly, Augusta's success was short-lived. Beginning in the early 1940s, her creative output dwindled sharply. Depression overcame her, and in a fit of frustration, she apparently destroyed much of her work. She spent the last seventeen years of her life in semi-seclusion in Saugerties, a small town in upstate New York. In failing health, she returned to New York City in 1962, where she died on March 26 at the age of seventy. Because she spent so many years in retirement, and because so little of her work survives, Augusta Savage is not well remembered today. But in the 1930s, she was a guiding light of the Harlem Renaissance.

Augusta Savage working
in her studio on *The Harp*

B
SAVAGE

Schroeder, Alan.

In her hands.

$19.95

DATE		

BAKER & TAYLOR